PIANO/VOCAL/CHORDS

THE BOY FROM OZ

Project Manager: CAROL CUELLAR
Book Art Layout: KEN REHM

CONTENTS

THE CONTINENTAL AMERICAN

Words and Music by
PETER ALLEN and
CAROLE BAYER SAGER

D7/F♯
F
C7/E
ply, we would drink__ foun - tains dry in a club_
Am7(♭5)/E♭
D7
Gm7
C/D
__ filled with sound. And
Cm7
F7
B♭maj7
B♭6
Cm7
F7
B♭maj7
bands that played_ to please__ me. We found a part - ner eas -
B♭6
Cm7
F7
B♭maj7
B♭6
y. Then, the name game was the on - ly__ game_ in town._

Chorus:
A♭
E♭/F
B♭
And then the nights would end at six A. M. You'd sleep all day and then start danc - ing a - gain,
E♭/B♭
F7
B♭
E♭
F7
Gm7
F7
N.C.
the first to see the end.
We did the
1.
F7
B♭
E♭maj9
con - ti - nen - tal A - mer - i - can.

2.
A♭maj7
D7
F7
con - ti - nen - tal A - mer -
B♭
A♭
G♭
A♭
i - can.
(Double-time feel)
Am7
Bm/A
Am7

Dm7
G7
Cmaj7
C6
Then the bands___ are play - ing to please me. You find_
Dm7
G7
Cmaj7
C6
Dm7
G7
Cmaj7
___ a part - ner real eas - y. C - 'mon, boy,
C6
B♭maj7
B♭6
B♭maj7
B♭6
you should have seen_ us then.___ When...___
D♭
E♭m/D♭
D♭
E♭m/D♭
N.C.
A♭7
N.C.
Nights would end at six A. M. Sleep all day,

Gb/Db Db Ebm7 Db/F Gb
then start danc-ing a-gain. First to see the end. Man-
Ab7
1. N.C. Db Gb Ab
2. N.C. Db A7
hat-tan pi-on-eers.
Chorus:
D G7 A7sus A7
Nights that end at six A. M. Sleep all day,
D Em/D
then start danc-ing a-gain. The first to see the end.

G7sus
N.C.
G7
We did the con - ti - nen - tal A - mer - i - can.
C
B♭
A♭
B♭
(Double-time feel)
(Inst. solo ad lib....
C
B♭
A♭
1.-6.
B♭
7.
B♭
C
(Inst. solo continues...

Verse 2:
All our clothes from France,
Soul Train taught us to dance.
We had smoke in our eyes.
In our eyes.
There were friends lost and found,
We were paradise-bound.
Some got lost, nobody cried.
But others took their places,
Always strange new faces.
Always one more chance to go around.
(To Chorus:)

ALL THE LIVES OF ME

Words and Music by
PETER ALLEN

D7
Em
B m7
And if you could see all the peo - ple, they're
And if you smile at some - one.
and if I make you feel tall
f
dim.
G7
C
G
ev - 'ry - one I ev - er was and ev - 'ry - one I ev - er will be,
Then I'll just be-come that one and throw in all the oth - ers for free,
af - ter know-in' all you know is real - ly on - ly all that you see,
mf
mp
To Coda
A
C (D bass)
1. G
G (sus 4)
2. G
G (sus 4)
all the lives of me. Noth - ing left to me.
all the lives of
all the lives of

G
Em
A (C♯bass)
Faults aren't things for hid - ing
f
Dmaj9
B m9
A11
on a shelf. And if you like who I am
mf
Dmaj7
B♭
B♭ (sus 4)
B♭
B♭ (sus 4)
now that's on - ly a re - flec - tion of ___ your -
D. S. 𝄋 al Coda 𝄌
Am7 (add D)
C (D bass)
G
G (sus 4)
self. All the games are
mp

Coda
G
G (sus 4)
B7 (sus 4)
B7
Em
me.
If you could see all the
f
B m7
G7
peo - ple;
they're
ev - 'ry - one I ev - er was
mf
C
A
C (D bass)
an' ev-'ry - one I ev - er will be
all the lives
mp
A (G bass)
C (G bass)
of me.

ARTHUR'S THEME
(Best That You Can Do)

Words and Music by
PETER ALLEN, CAROLE BAYER SAGER,
CHRISTOPHER CROSS and BURT BACHARACH

G7
C
F
her, some-one who turns your heart a - round, and
pleas - es. All of his life, his mas - ter's toys, and
B♭
E7sus4
E7
A
next thing you know, you're clos - in' down the town.
deep in his heart, he's just, he's just a boy.
E/A
A
A/C♯
Dm7
G7
Wake up and she's still with you,
Liv - in' his life one day at a time, he's
C
F
B♭
e - ven though you left her way a-cross town. You're won - der - in' to your -
show - ing him - self a real - ly good time. He's laugh - in' a - bout the

E7sus4
E7
A
E/A
A
A/C#
self, hey, what - 've I found?
way they want him to be.
Dmaj7
E/D
4fr.
D
Amaj7
When you get caught be-tween the moon and New York Cit - y,
Bm7
A/B
Bm7
I know it's cra - zy, but it's true.
A
A/C#
Dmaj7
If you get caught be - tween the

E/D
4fr.
D
C#m7
4fr.
F#7sus4
F#7
moon and New York Cit - y, the
Bm7
best that you can do, the best that you can do
1.
2.
D. S. and fade
D/A
A
A/C#
A
A/C#
is fall_ in love.___

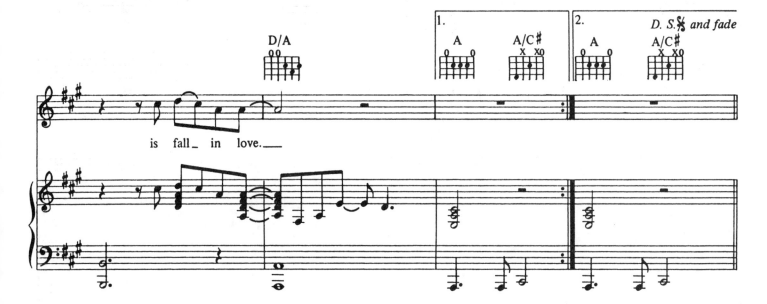

BI-COASTAL

Words and Music by
PETER ALLEN, DAVID FOSTER and TOM KEANE

Moderately Disco beat
F/G G7 F/G B♭/D Am/E Gm/F D7+5/F♯
3fr.
mf
F/G G7 F/G G7
You used to live in New York Cit - y then you moved to L. A.,
You hit the streets at mid - night, still danc - in' af - ter down,
You can al - ways hear me sing - ing oh, say can you see
(with pedal throughout)
F/G G7 F/G G7
but you still miss the streets where you used to play.
but some - thin' seems to be miss - in'. Just what are you run - nin' from?
from the tow - ers of Man - hat - tan to the hills of Bev - er - ly.

G/A
A7
G/A
So you hur - ry on back there, you
Do you like your love in the dark, or
All those girls on T. V. mov - ies,
A7
B♭/C
C7
e - ven leave your pool and your car,
on - ly to find you no long -
laid out in the sun?
When you can't make up
all those boys on Broad-way.
When you can't make up
B♭/C
1.
C7
F/G
er be - long.
Fool, don't you know what you are?
your mind,
your mind,

2.
Db/Eb
Bb/C
Bbm7
Cm7
don't you know what you be-come?
you know you'd go ei-ther way.
Bi - coast - al, miss
Fm9
Ab/Bb
4fr.
Bbm7
the nat - 'ral speed of the cit - y.
Cm7
Fm9
To Coda
Bi - coast - al Cal - i - for - nia's fine if you're pret - ty.
Ab/Bb
4fr.
Db/Eb
D.S. (no repeats) al Coda

Coda
A♭/B♭
4fr.
B♭m7
Cm7
Bi - coast - al, when both are so much fun; —
Fm9
A♭/B♭
4fr.
D♭/E♭
B♭m7
— tell me why — do you have to pick one? —
Repeat and fade
Cm7
Fm9
A♭/B♭
4fr.
B♭m7
Bi - coast - al.

DON'T CRY OUT LOUD

Words and Music by
PETER ALLEN and CAROLE BAYER SAGER

D
F♯m(C♯bass)
Bm
F♯m
wire. I know a lot a-bout her 'cause you see, ba-
Bm7
E7
Em7(A bass)
A7
D
A(C♯bass)
-by is an aw-ful lot like me. We don't cry out
Bm
Em
Em(maj7)
Em7(A bass)
A7
loud, we keep it in-side, learn how to hide our feel-ings.
D
A(C♯bass)
Bm
Em
Em(maj7)
Fly high and proud, and if you should fall, re-mem-ber you

Em7 (A bass)
B maj7
Em7 (A bass)
al - most had it all.
D
F♯ m7
Ba - by saw them when they pulled the big - top down, they
Em7
Em7 (A bass)
D
left be - hind her dreams a - mong the lit - ter.
F♯ m7
And the dif-f'rent kind of love she thought she'd found, was

Em7
Em7 (A bass)
D
F♯ m7 (C♯ bass)
Bm
noth-in' more__ than saw-dust and some glit - ter. But ba - by can't be bro - ken 'cause you see,__
F♯ m
B m7
E7
__ she has__ the fi - nest teach - er,______
Em7 (A bass)
D
A (C♯ bass)
Bm
me. An' I taught her: don't cry out loud, just keep it in -
Em
Em (maj7)
Em7 (A bass)
A7
D
A (C♯ bass)
side, learn__ how to hide your feel - ings. Fly high and

Bm
Em
Em (maj7)
Em7 (A bass)
B♭ 7
proud, and if you should fall, tell me you al - most had it.
E♭
B♭ (D bass)
Cm
Fm
Fm (maj7)
ff
Don't cry out loud, just keep it in - side, learn how to
Fm7 (B♭ bass)
B♭ 7
E♭
B♭ (D bass)
Cm
hide your feel - ings. Fly high and proud, and if you should
Fm
Fm (maj7)
Fm7 (B♭ bass)
B♭ 7
E♭
B♭ (D bass)
fall, re - mem - ber you al - most had it all. Don't

Cm
Fm
Fm(maj7)
Fm7(B♭bass)
cry out loud, just keep it in - side, learn how to hide your feel - ings.
E♭
B♭(D bass)
Cm
Fm
Fm(maj7)
Fly high and proud, and if you should fall, well ba - by you
Fm7(B♭bass)
G7
Cm
Cm(B♭bass)
A♭
A♭(B♭bass)
E♭
al - most, you al - most had it all.
D
A(C♯bass)
Bm7
Em
Em(maj7)
Em7(A bass)
D. S. 𝄋 and fade
mf

DON'T WISH TOO HARD

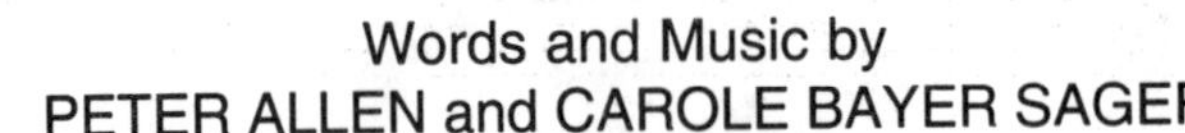

Words and Music by
PETER ALLEN and CAROLE BAYER SAGER

Moderate Disco beat

Tacet

mf

Emaj7

Don't wish too hard for what you want or
My poor heart's re - peat - in' it can't stand the beat - in'

Background vocal ad lib

G (A bass)

then you might get it, and
that it's been tak - in'. I can't

F♯m7
then when you get it
tell when you're fak - in'
B11
you might find you did - n't want it at all.
ev - 'ry time you're mak - in' love to me.
B7-9
Emaj7
And don't go look -
One day soon
in for love to come or
I'm gon - na change my tune and with -

G(A bass)
then it might find you,
out hes - i - tat - in'
F♯ m7
and then when it finds you
I'll be leav - in' you wait - in'.
To Coda
B11
you might wish that you had
You'll be wait - in' at the
G♯7
nev - er been born.
gate for me.
Oo,
Oh,

C♯
C♯ maj7
how I ___ wished ___ for you and now you're __ here; ___
Then you'll _ wish ___ for me and I won't be here. ___
how I ___ wished ___ for you and now you're __ here; ___
C♯ 7
now I wish that you would
So long, dar - lin', I'll just
now I wish that you would
F♯ maj7
B11
dis - ap - pear ___ and go a - way.
dis - ap - pear ___ and go a - way.
dis - ap - pear ___ and go a - way.

No chord
1.2.
3.
D. S. (lyric 1) al Coda
Oh,
Coda
B11
C♯m6
you'll find what you real - ly want - ed and what
you real - ly wished for you nev - er real - ly
Amaj7 (B bass)
Emaj7
want - ed at all.

N.C.
Bom, bom, bom,
Emaj7
Repeat (vocal ad lib) and fade
don't wish too hard,
and
Repeat and fade
G (A base)
don't go look - in'.
No,

EVERYTHING OLD IS NEW AGAIN

Words and Music by
PETER ALLEN and CAROLE BAYER SAGER

Moderately
Tacet
mf
C
D9
C
C (B♭bass)
A7
When trum - pets were mel - low and ev - 'ry gal on - ly had one fel - low,
your Long Is - land Jazz Age par - ties, wait - er, bring us some more Ba - car - dis,
Don't throw the past a - way, you might need it some rain - y day.
To Coda
D9
G7 (sus 4)
G7
C
C (B♭bass)
F (A bass)
A♭ 7 (-5)
no need to re - mem - ber when 'cause ev - 'ry - thing old is
we'll or - der now what they or - dered then 'cause ev - 'ry - thing old is
Dreams can come true a - gain, when ev - 'ry - thing old is

1.
G7
C
C
F(A bass)
A♭7(-5)
G7
C
new a - gain.
Danc - in' at
2.
G7
C
E7
B♭7(-5)
new a - gain.
Get out your white suit your tap shoes and tails,
A7
D13
let's go back - wards when all else fails.
And mov - ie stars you
G13
G7(+5)
D. S. 𝄋 al Coda
thought were long dead now are framed be - side your bed.

Coda
G7
C
C (B♭ bass)
F (A bass)
A♭ 7 (-5)
G7
C
new a - gain.
Get out
E7
your white suit, your tap shoes and tails.
A7
D13
Put it in back - ward when for - ward fails.
But leave Gret - a
G7
Tacet
G7
Gar - bo a - lone, be a mov - ie star on your own. And

E♭
F7
E♭
don't __ throw the past a - way, __ you might need it some
Gm7
C7
F7
B♭7
rain - y day. __ Dreams can come true a - gain, __ when
E♭
E♭(D♭bass)
A♭(C bass)
B7(-5)
B♭7
E♭
E♭
A♭
B7
ev - 'ry - thing old is new a - gain. __
B♭7
E♭
Cm7
F7
B♭7
E♭
I might fall __ in love with __ you a - gain. __
freely
a tempo

I GO TO RIO

Words and Music by
PETER ALLEN and ADRIENNE ANDERSON

E7 (sus 4)
E7
My oh me oh, I go wild
There on the hot sand and in a bun-
E7 (sus 4)
E7
A (add 9)
A
and then I have to do the Sam - ba
ga - low while mon - keys play a - bove - a
A (add 9)
A
and La Bam - ba. Now I'm
we'll make love - a. Now I'm
Gmaj7 (A bass)
not the kind of per - son with a pas - sion - ate per -
not the type to let vi - bra - tions trig - ger my im -

Dmaj9
sua - sion for danc - in' or ro -
ag - i - na - tion eas - i - ly. You know that's
Fmaj7 (G bass)
Gmaj7 (A bass)
manc - in'. But I give in to the rhy -
just not me. But I turn in - to a ti -
thm and my feet fol - low the beat - ing of my
ger ev - 'ry time I get be - side the one I
F♯7 (sus 4)
F♯7
Tacet
heart.
love.
Woah, when my

E7(sus 4)
E7
E7(sus 4)
E7
ba - by,
when my ba - by smiles at me
A(add 9)
A
I go to Ri - o
de Ja - nei -
A(add 9)
A
E7(sus 4)
E7
ro.
I'm a Sal - sa fel - low.
E7(sus 4)
E7
When my ba - by smiles at me the sun

G♯m7(-5)
C♯7
F♯m7
lights ___ up my life and
B7
I feel free at last, ___
E7(sus 4)
E7
A(sus 4)
A
what a blast. ___
A(sus 4)
A
1.
When my ba -

Vocal ad lib

When my baby
When my baby smiles at me
I go to Rio de Janeiro
It's when I go to Rio
Rio de Janeiro

I HONESTLY LOVE YOU

Words and Music by
PETER ALLEN and JEFF BARRY

Slowly
8va
8va

B♭
F (B♭ bass)
May-be I hang a-round here a lit-tle more than I should we
you don't have to an - swer I see it in your eyes
rit.

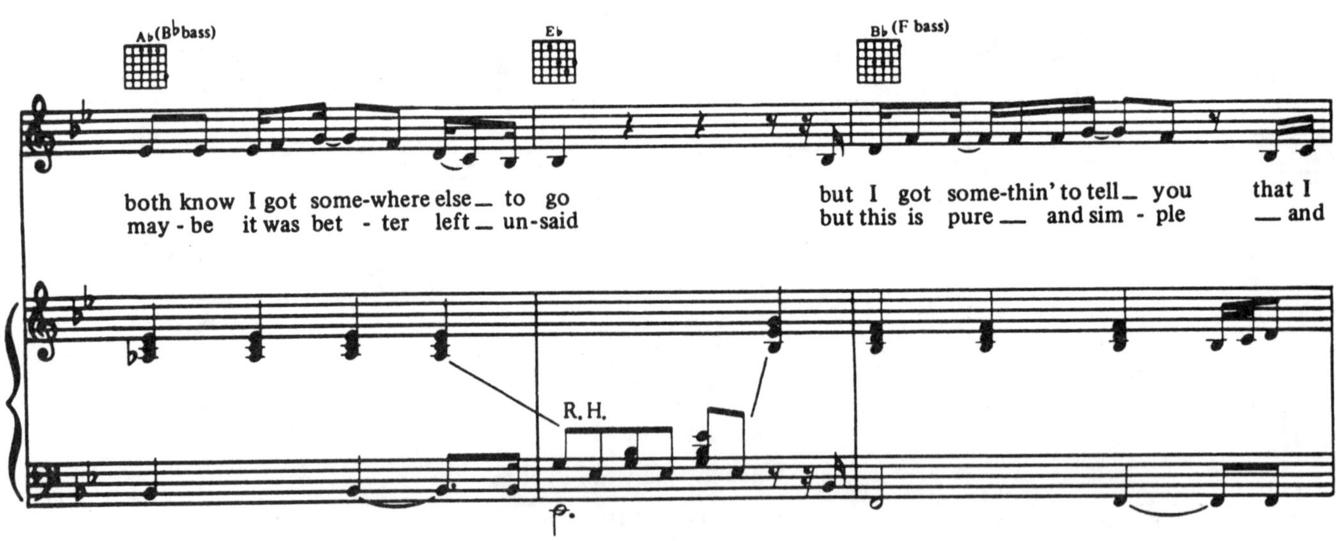
A♭(B♭ bass)
E♭
B♭ (F bass)
both know I got some-where else to go but I got some-thin' to tell you that I
may-be it was bet - ter left un-said but this is pure and sim - ple and
R.H.

C7
E♭
B♭(D bass)
Cm7
F7
never thought I would but I be-lieve you real-ly ought to know
you must re - a-lize that it's com-in' from my heart and not my head
B♭
F (B♭bass)
E♭ (B♭bass)
1. B♭
I love you
I hon-est-ly love you.
F (B♭bass)
E♭ (B♭bass)
2. B♭
F (B♭bass)
(B♭bass)
A♭
B♭
you.
E♭
F (E♭bass)
Dm7
Gm7
Cm7
F7
I'm not tryin' to make you feel un - comf'-ta-ble
I'm not tryin' to make you an - y - thing at

B♭ Am7 D7 Gm7 B♭(F bass) F (E♭bass) E♭
all but this feel-ing does-n't come a-long ev-'ry day and you
E♭ B♭ (D bass) Cm7 Cm7 (F bass) B♭
should-n't blow the chance when you got the chance to say I love you
F (B♭bass) E♭(B♭bass) E♭m(B♭bass)
SPOKEN: I love you
I hon-est-ly love
B♭ F♯7 B
you.
If we both were born in an-

F♯ (B bass)
A (B bass)
E
oth - er place and time this mo - ment might be end-ing with a kiss but
B (F♯ bass)
C♯7
E
B (D♯ bass)
there you are with yours and here I am with mine so I guess we'll just be leav - ing it at
C♯m7
C♯m7 (F♯ bass)
B
F♯ (B bass)
F (B bass)
this I love you I hon-est - ly love
B
F♯ (B bass)
E (B bass)
B
you I hon-est - ly love you.
F♯ (B bass)
E (B bass)
B
8va
rit.

I STILL CALL AUSTRALIA HOME

Words and Music by
PETER ALLEN

F
A7/E
Dm
G7/B
F/C
mat - ter how far or how wide I roam, I still call Aus -
Gm7/C C7
F
B♭
Am
C7
tra - lia home.
F VERSE II
A7
Dm
F F'sus F
B♭
I'm al - ways trav' - lin', I love be - ing free, And so I keep
Dm7/A
G7
Gm7/C
F
A7/E
leav - ing the sun and the sea, But my heart lies wait - ing

Dm
G7/B
F/C
Gm7/C C7
F
o - ver___ the foam, I still call___ Aus - tra - lia home.
E
Am
Am(maj7)/G♯
Am7/G
All the sons and daugh - ters spin - ning 'round the
Am6/F♯
Dm7
G7
C
E
world, A - way from___ their fam - 'ly and friends. But
Am
Am/G♯
Am7/G
Am6/F♯
Dm7/G
as the world gets old - er and cold - er, It's good to know where your

Gm7
C7
F VERSE III
A7
jour - ney ends.
But some - day we'll all be to -
rall.
a tempo
Dm
F Fsus F
B♭
Dm7/A
G7
geth - er once more. When all of the ships come back to the
Gm7/C
F
A7/E
Dm
G7/B
shore. I re - al - ize some - thing I've al - - ways known,
F/C
Gm7/C C7
F
B♭
Am
C7
I still call Aus - tra - lia home.
D.S. 𝄋 al 𝄌, then Coda

Gm7/C CODA *
F
A7/E
Dm
G7/B
But no mat - ter how far or how wide I roam, I
F/C
Gm7/C C7
F/C
Gm7/C C7
F/C
still call Aus - tra - lia, I still call Aus - tra - lia, I still call Aus -
Gm7/C C7
F
A7/E
Dm
1 Gm7/C
tra - lia home.
But no
2 Gm7/C
F
A7/E
Dm
Gm7/C
INSTRUMENTAL ONLY
Repeat and fade out

I'D RATHER LEAVE WHILE I'M IN LOVE

Words and Music by
PETER ALLEN and CAROLE BAYER SAGER

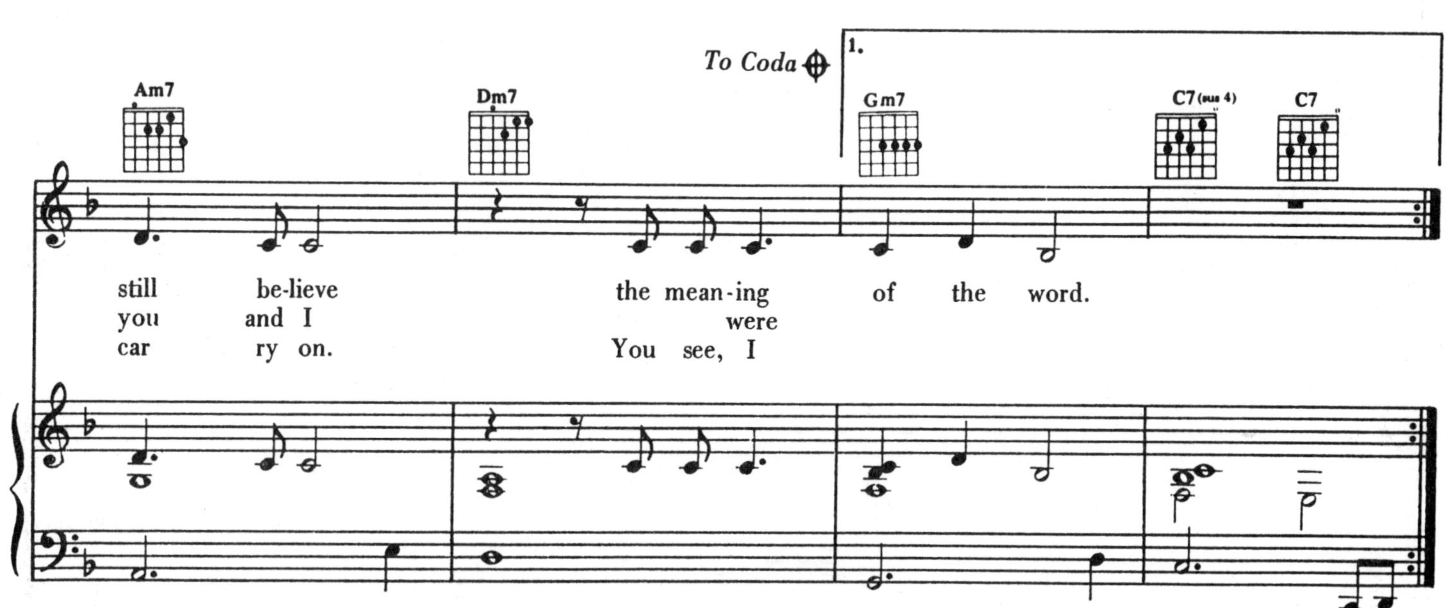

I'd Rather Leave While I'm in Love - 5 - 1

2.
Gm7
A7 (sus 4)
A7
D
D (F♯bass)
nev - er meant to end.
Too man - y times I've seen the
Em7
A7 (sus 4)
A7
D
D (F♯bass)
rose die on the vine.
And some-bod - y's heart gets brok - en
Em7
A7 (sus 4)
A7
E♭
Cm7
Fm7
u - sual - ly it's mine.
I don't wan-na take the chance of be - ing hurt a -
G7 (sus 4)
G7
C (sus 4)
C
C11
D. S. 𝄋 al Coda
gain and you and I can't say good - bye.

Coda
Gm7
C7 (sus 4)
F
F (A bass)
need my fan - ta - sy.
I still be - lieve
Gm7
C7 (sus 4)
F
F (A bass)
B♭ maj7
it's best to leave while I'm in love.
C (B♭ bass)
Am7
Dm7
Gm7
A7 (sus 4)
A7
D
D (F♯ bass)
Em7
A7 (sus 4)
A7
Too man - y times I've seen the rose die on the vine.

D
D (F♯ bass)
Em7
A7
A7
And some - bod - y's heart gets brok - en u - sual - ly it's mine.
F
Dm7
Gm7
A7 (sus 4)
A7
I don't wan - na take the chance of be - ing hurt a - gain. And
D (sus 4)
D
D11
you and I can't say good - bye.
G
G (B bass)
Cmaj7
D (C bass)
So if you wake and find me gone hey babe, just

Bm7
Em7
Am7
D7 (sus 4)
D7
car - ry on.
You see, I
need my fan - ta - sy.
G (D bass)
D7 (sus 4)
B7 (+5)
I still be - lieve
it's best to leave
while I'm in
Em7
Am7
D7 (sus 4)
love.
I'd rath - er leave while I'm in
rit.
G
G (B bass)
Cmaj7
F7
G (add A)
love.
a tempo

IF YOU WERE WONDERING

Words and Music by
PETER ALLEN

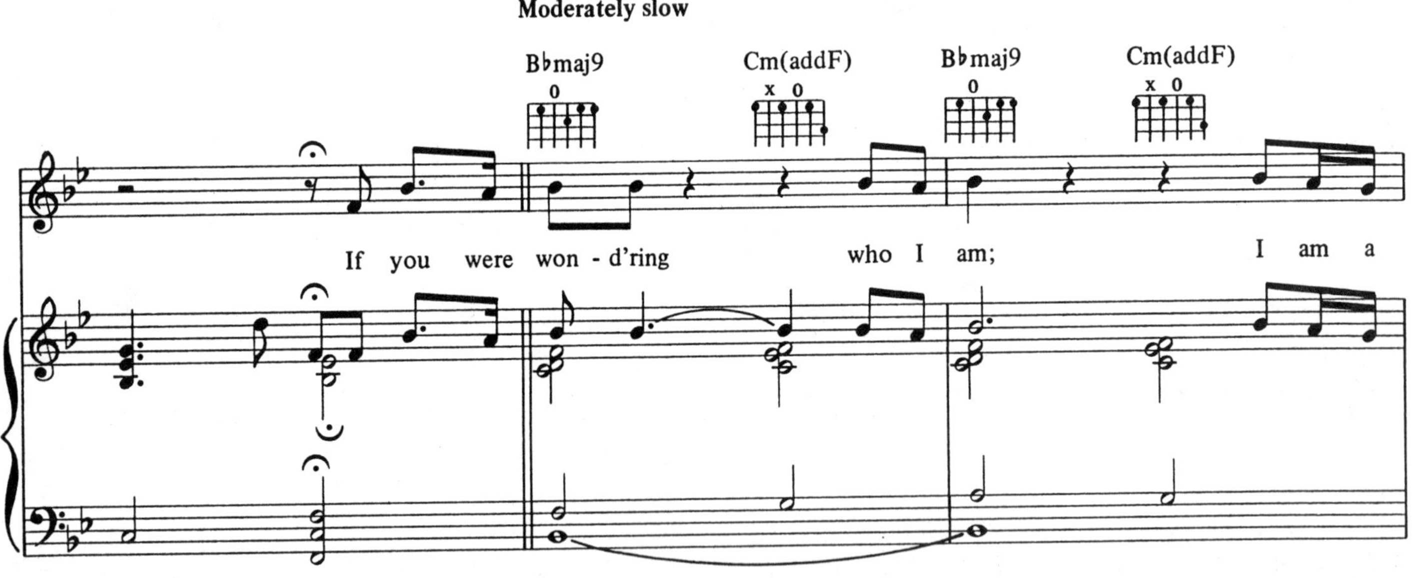

B♭maj9
Cm(addF)
Dm7
man, just like an - y oth - er man, un - like an - y oth - er
E♭/F
Dm/F
man. If you were won - d'ring who I was; I was a
molto rit.
a tempo
Fm7
B♭13
6fr.
boy, just an or - di - nar - y boy start - ing out on some great mys - ter-
With a beat
E♭(addF)
3fr.
Gm7
C9
y. On the road, when I had no choice, I
mf

Fmaj7
Fmaj7+5
F6
D7-9
Gm7
Gm7/F
wait - ed out a cen - tur - y. I took a load un - til I
Em7-5
A7-9
Dm9
G7-5 -9
To Coda
Cm9/F
found my voice. There's noth - ing wrong with be - in' me.
Tacet
Bb maj9
Cm(addF)/F
If you were won - d'ring who I

B♭maj9 Cm(addF)/F B♭maj9 Cm(addF) B♭maj9 Cm(addF)/F
love, I love you. That's all I have to do 'cause I'm a
B♭maj9 Cm(addF)/F Dm7 Dm(addE) 2fr. Cm7(addF)
man just like an - y oth - er man, un - like an -
Slower
Cm7/F 8fr. B♭maj9 Cm(addF)/F B♭maj9 Cm(addF)/F Tacet
y oth - er man.

D.S. al Coda
On the
Coda
Cm9
Bb maj9
Cm(addF)/F
Bb maj9
Cm(addF)/F
be - in' me. If you were won - d'ring who I love, I love
Bb maj9
Cm(addF)/F
Bb maj9
D7-9
4fr.
Gm7
3fr.
you. 'Cause that's all I have to do. I'm a man, just like
Dm7
Cm7(addF)
Cm7/F
8fr.
an - y oth - er man, un - like an - y oth - er man.

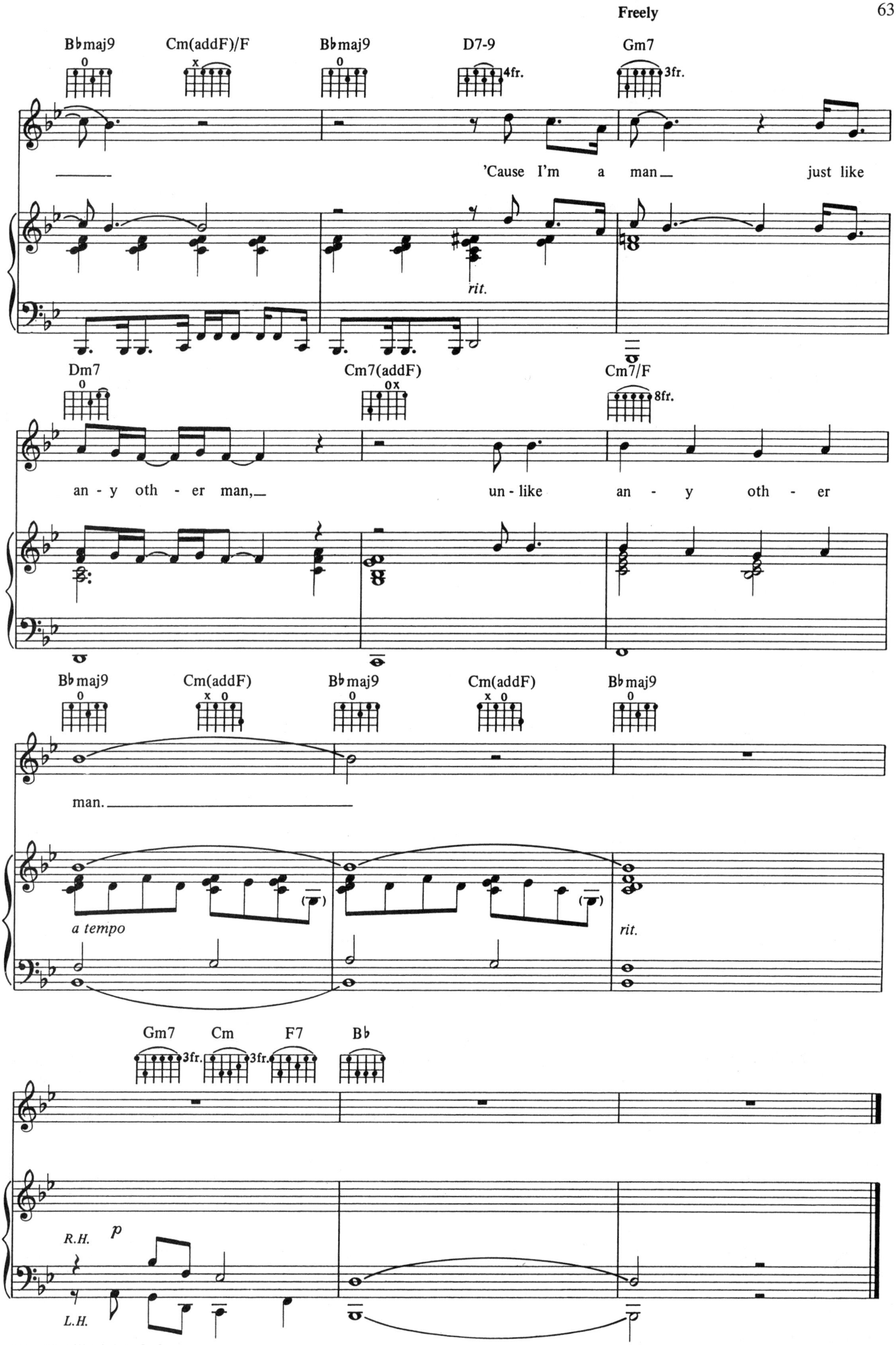

Freely

B♭maj9 Cm(addF)/F B♭maj9 D7-9 Gm7

'Cause I'm a man just like

rit.

Dm7 Cm7(addF) Cm7/F

an - y oth - er man, un - like an - y oth - er

B♭maj9 Cm(addF) B♭maj9 Cm(addF) B♭maj9

man.

a tempo

rit.

Gm7 Cm F7 B♭

R.H. *p*

L.H.

LOVE CRAZY

Words and Music by
PETER ALLEN and
ADRIENNE ANDERSON

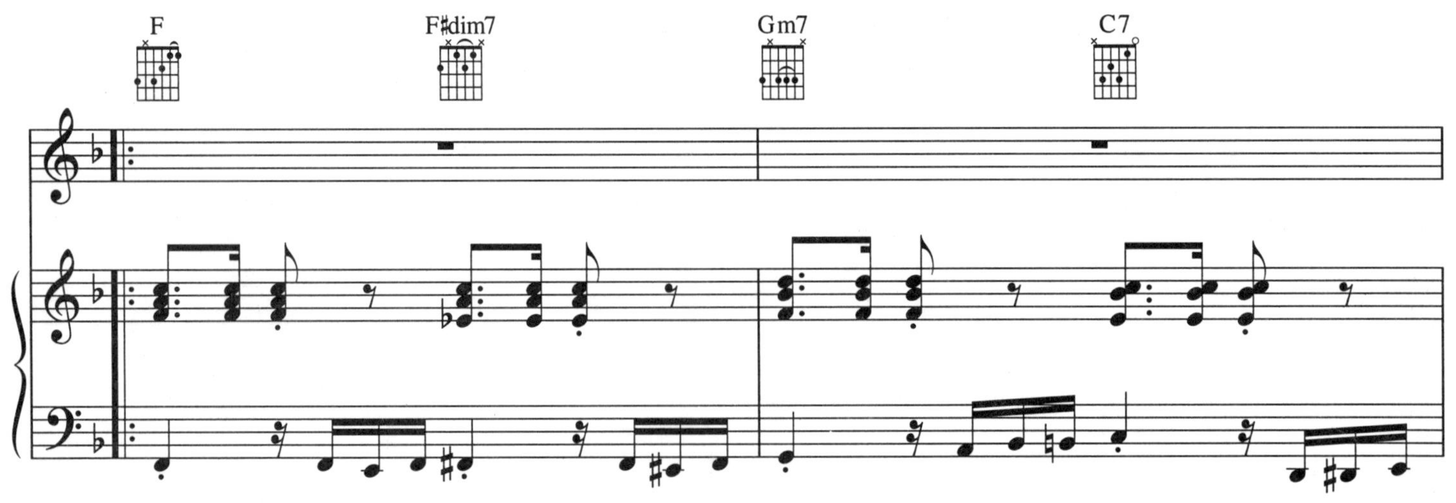

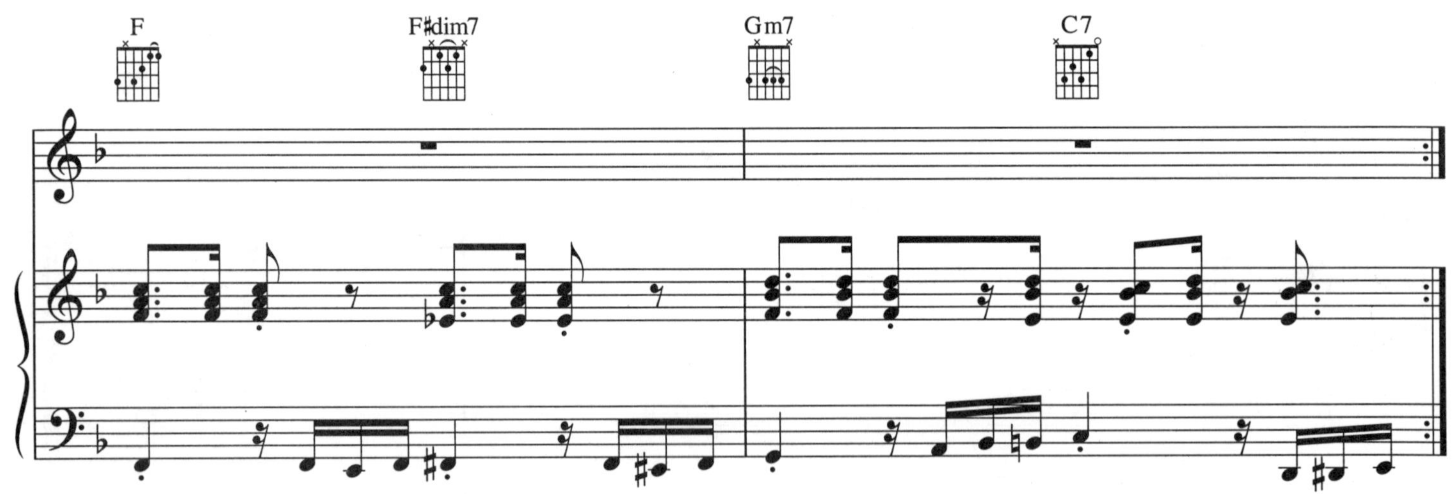

F
F♯dim7
Gm7
C7
F
F♯dim7
Gm7
C7
F
G7
Verse:
C
C♯dim7
Dm7
G7
1. Lis-ten to the mu - sic in__ your__ voice.___ Oh, don't you hear the mu - sic ev - 'ry - where?
2. Lis-ten to the mu - sic in__ the wa - ter. Don't you see its worth be - fore your eyes?
C
C♯dim7
Dm7
G7
Catch the mel - o - dy a-bove the noise,_ you can feel it puls - ing__ through the air.
Don't it fill you up and full__ of won - der how the sun can set and the moon_ can rise?_

Gm7
C7
Fmaj7
A♭/B♭
E♭maj7
The whole world is buzz - ing and the light from_ the sun__ com-bined with ev - 'ry -
The whole_ world_ is__ buzz-ing and the light______ from_ the stars_ com-bined with ev - 'ry -
F/G
N.C.
Chorus:
Fm7
B♭7
thing all makes me
thing all makes me
love cra - zy.
Gm7
C7
Fm7
B♭7
Liv - ing is a cra - zy thing._
Love cra - zy,
Gm7
1.
C7
N.C.
2.
C7
N.C.
en - er - gy is ev - 'ry - thing.
'ry - thing.
Hey,

Chorus:
F♯m7
B7
G♯m7
C♯7
love cra - zy, liv - ing is a cra - zy thing.
F♯m7
B7
G♯m7
C♯7
N.C.
Love cra - zy, en - er - gy is ev - 'ry - thing.
F
F♯dim7
Gm7
C7
F
F♯dim7
Gm7
C7
F
Don't you know the whole

Am7
D9
Gmaj7
B♭/C
C9
Fmaj7
world is buzz - ing and the light of the sun com-bined with ev - 'ry -
G7
N.C.
C7
thing, oh, makes me love cra - zy.
D7
Gm7
Liv - ing is a cra - zy thing.
Love cra - zy,
en - er - gy is ev - 'ry - thing.
Love cra - zy,

Am7
D7
Gm7
C7
liv - ing is a cra - zy thing.
Love cra - zy,
Am7
D7
en - er - gy is ev - 'ry - thing.
F
F♯dim7
Gm7
C7
F
F♯dim7
Gm7
C7
F

LOVE DON'T NEED A REASON

(What We Don't Have Is Time)

Words and Music by
PETER ALLEN, MICHAEL L. CALLEN
and MARSHA MALAMET

Fmaj7/G F6/G F/G G7 C(addD)
might just miss the one who's stand - ing there. So in -
they to know it's not who's wrong or right? It's
G7sus4 Dm7 G7
stead of pass - ing by show the some - one that you care in -
just an - oth - er way. And it's not a - bout a fight, it's
Am Am(maj7) C/D D7
stead of ask - ing "Why, why me? And why you? Why
just I wan - na stay with you to the end, with
Dm7 Em7 Fmaj7 G7 C Em Fmaj7
not we two!"
you, my friend.
'Cause love don't need a rea - son.

F♯m7 B9 Em7 B♭/C C7 F G/B Am Em7/G
Love don't al - ways rhyme. And love is all we
F Fm6/A♭ Fm6/G 1. C C/E G7sus4
have for now. What we don't have is time. If you
2. C C(addD)/E Fmaj7 Em7
time. I'll hold you close, time can't tear us a - part.
Fmaj7 Bm7-5 E7 Am Fmaj7
I will stand by you. We've got to start with the

Em7
D/E
G/A
A
G/A
Em/B
A/C♯
beat of one heart. Together we will see this through. 'Cause
D
Dmaj7/F♯
Gmaj7
C♯7sus4
F♯m7
C/D
D7
love don't need a reason. Love's never a crime. And
Gmaj7
A/C♯
Bm
F♯m7/A
G
Gm6/B♭
Gm6/A
love is all we have for now. What we don't have, what
D
D/F♯
Gmaj7
G/A
D
we don't have is time.
rit.

NOT THE BOY NEXT DOOR

Words and Music by
PETER ALLEN and DEAN PITCHFORD

Bbsus4 Bb
Ab9/11 Ab9
Ab9/11 Ab9
Bbsus4 Bb
Bb Bbsus4 Bb
Ab9/11 Ab9
Ab9/11 Ab9
Com - in' home used to feel so good. I'm a stran - ger now in my
You've been sav - in' those sou - ve - nirs, fad - ed pho - to - graphs from my
Bb
Bbsus4 Bb
Ab9/11 Ab9
neigh - bor - hood. I've seen the world at a fast - er pace and I'm
fool - ish years. We made plans, but they're wear - in' thin, and they
Ab9/11 Ab9
Bb
Dm7/A Gm7
F
com - in' now from a dif - f'rent place. Though I may look the same way to you,
won't work out 'cause I don't fit in. And those mem - 'ries will just weigh me down,
4fr.
3fr.

E♭maj7 F/G

un - der - neath there is some - bod - y new.
'cause I got no place to keep 'em up - town.

C Dm7 F/G

I am not the boy next door. I don't be - long like I

C G/B Am7 Dm7

did be - fore. Noth - in' ev - er seems like it used to be. You can

F/G G Am7

have your dreams, but you can't have me. I can't go back there

D7/F♯
Gm
B♭/F
F
an - y - more_ 'cause I am not the boy next_ door._
1.
B♭sus4
B♭
A♭9/11
A♭9
2.

Bbsus4
Bb
Ab9/11
Ab9
4fr.
3
3
Ab9/11
Ab9
4fr.
3
Bbsus4
Bb
3
Bbsus4
Bb

Ab9/11
Ab9
4fr.
Bbsus4
Bb
Dm7/A
Gm7
3fr.
F
Ebmaj7
F/G
D.S. and fade
And I'm sor - ry for just be - in'
me, but if you'd look past the past you could see that ...

QUIET PLEASE, THERE'S A LADY ON STAGE

Words and Music by
PETER ALLEN and CAROLE BAYER SAGER

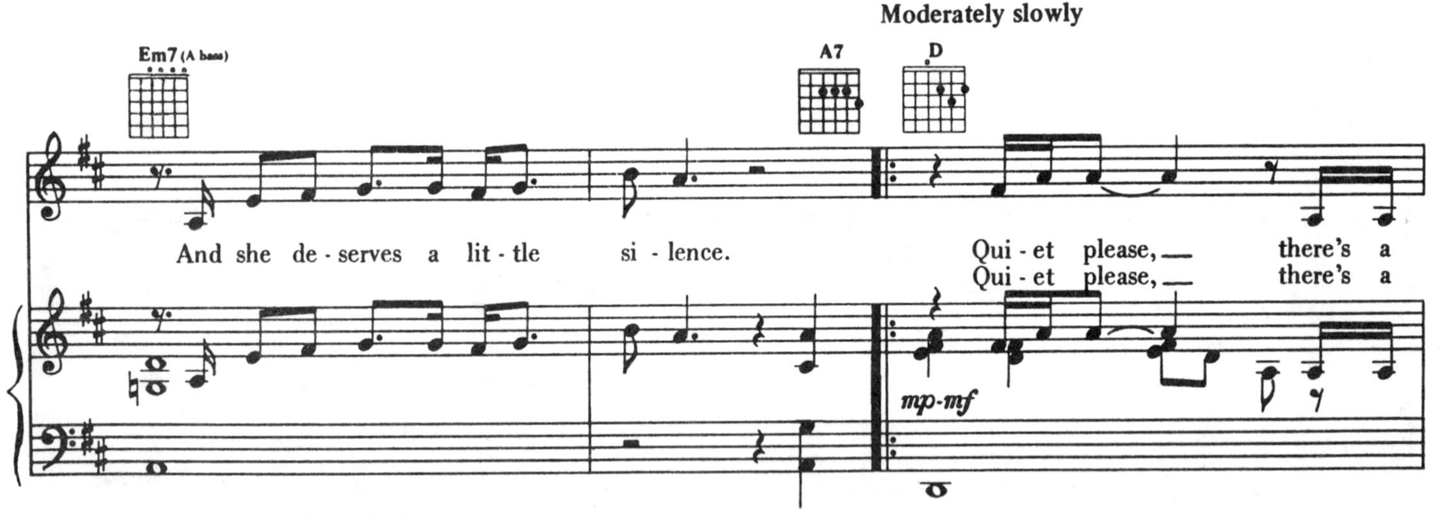

A (D bass)
Am7
D7
G (B bass)
Gm (B♭ bass)
wom - an up there. And she's been hon-est through her songs long be - fore your con-scious-ness was
per - son up there who's sing - in' of the sins that none of us could bear to
D (A bass)
E9
A7(sus 4)
A7
raised. Now does-n't that de - serve a lit - tle praise? So
hear for our-self. Give her your re - spect if noth-in' else. And
Rhythmically
F
Fmaj7
put your hands to - geth - er and help her a - long, all that's
Cm7
F7
B♭
A
B♭
Dm7
left of the sing - er's, all that's left of the song.
Stand for the o -
Rise to the oc -
Stand for the o -

G9
Gm9
Am7
To Coda
1.
B♭ maj7
A (sus 4)
va - tion
ca - sion
va - tion
and give her one last cel - e - bra - tion.
2.
B♭ maj7
A (sus 4)
Delicately
D
A (D bass)
cel - e - bra - tion.
Qui-et please, there's a la - dy on stage.
G (D bass)
Gm (D bass)
D
Con-duc-tor, turn the fi - nal page. When it's o - ver we can
D. S. al Coda
E9
Em7 (A bass)
Tacet
A7
G (B bass)
C7
all go home, but she lives on on the stage a - lone. So

Coda
B♭ maj7
C♯ 7
F♯
cel - e - bra - tion. Put your hands to - geth - er and
F♯ maj7
C♯ m7
F♯ 7
B
A♯
B
help her a - long, all that's left of the sing-er's, all that's left of the song.
D♯ m7
G♯9
G♯ m7
A♯ m7
Rise for the o - va - tion and give her one last
B maj7
C♯ 7
F♯
F♯ maj7
cel - e - bra - tion. Put your hands to - geth-er, help her a - long, all that's

C♯m7
F♯7
B
D7
left of the sing - er's, all that's left of the song.
G
Repeat ad lib and fade
Gmaj7
Put your hands to - geth - er, help her a - long;
all that's
let's just
Repeat ad lib and fade
Dm7
G7
C
Em7
left of the sing - er's, all that's left of the song.
stay here all night and let's sing ev - 'ry song.
Won't you
Stand for the o -
rise to the oc -
A9
Am9
B m7
Cmaj7
D7
va - tion,
ca - sion,
and won't you give her one last cel - e - bra - tion.

WALTZING MATILDA

Words by
A.B. "Banjo" PATERSON

Music by
MARIE COWAN

Moderately ♩ = 104
F♯m
B 7
E
til - da, with me.
mf
Chorus:
E 7
A
B♭dim7
Waltz - ing Ma - til - da,
Waltz - ing Ma - til - da.
E
C♯7
F♯m7
B 7
You'll come a - waltz - ing, Ma - til - da, with me.
And he
E
G♯7
C♯m
A
sang as he watched
and wait - ed till his bil - ly boiled.

E G♯m F♯m B7 E

You'll come a - waltz - ing, Ma - til - da, with me.

Verse 2:

G♯7 C♯m A

2. Down came a squat - ter, mount - ed on a thor-ough - bred.

E G♯m D B

Down came the troop - ers, one, two, three.

E G♯7 C♯m A

Where's that jol - ly jum - buck you've got in your tuck - er bag?

E
G♯m
F♯m
B7
Em
You'll come a - waltz - ing, Ma - til - da, with me.
Verse 3:
B7/D♯
G/D
C♯m7(♭5)
3. Up jumped the swag - man, sprang in - to the bil - la - bong.
Em
B
Em
B7/D♯
You'll nev - er take me a - live, said he. And his ghost may be heard as you
G/D
C♯m7(♭5)
Em
C7
pass_ by that bil - la-bong.

Chorus:

F F7 B♭ Bdim7

Waltz - ing Ma - til - da, Waltz - ing Ma - til - da,

F D7 Gm7 C C♯

you'll come a - waltz - ing, Ma - til - da, with me.__

F♯ F♯7 B Cdim7

Waltz - ing Ma - til - da, Waltz - ing Ma - til - da,

F♯ D♯7 G♯m C♯ D

you'll come a - waltz - ing, Ma - til - da, with me.__

G
G7
C
C♯dim7
Waltz - ing Ma - til - da, Waltz - ing Ma - til - da,
G
E7
Am7
D7
you'll come a - waltz - ing, Ma - til - da, with me. And his
G
B7
Em
C
D
C
ghost may be heard as you pass by that bil - la - bong.
G
Bm/F♯
You'll come a - waltz - ing,

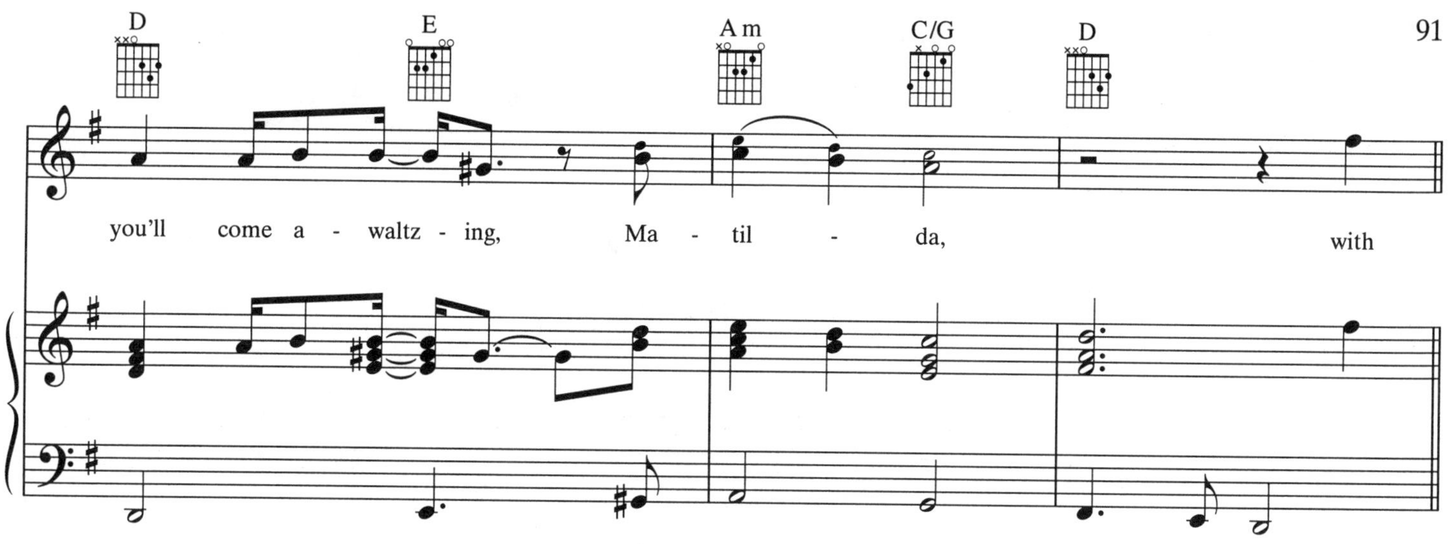
D
E
Am
C/G
D
you'll come a - waltz - ing, Ma - til - da, with

G
me.
You'll come a - waltz - ing.
You'll come a - waltz - ing.

Repeat ad lib. and fade
You'll come a - waltz - ing.
You'll come a - waltz - ing.

SHE LOVES TO HEAR THE MUSIC

Words and Music by
PETER ALLEN and
CAROLE BAYER SAGER

F♯m7 B7 D A/C♯

is writ-ten on an al - bum sleeve. And she can tell you who is hot and

Bm7 E7sus E7

who will make it and who___ will not.___ 'Cause she

Chorus:

Am7 G♯dim7

loves to hear___ the mu - sic, she's got ev - 'ry lyr - ic down.___

Am/G F♯m7(♭5)

She loves to hear them sing, she's got the great - est ears___ in town.

Dm7
G
Dm7
G
She's there at ev - 'ry stu - di - o,
there ain't a pop star she don't know.
Am
G
Fmaj7
And some - times, they take her home,
but she al -
Dm7
Em7
A(9)
Asus2 sus4
A(9)
Asus2 sus4
ways wakes up a - lone.
2. The
Verse 2:
A
D
E7
men that want to mar - ry her
can nev - er sat - is - fy,

A
A/C♯
D
A/C♯
Bm7
E7sus
E7
the in - ner rhy-thms that__ she hears__ are all that keep__ her high.__
F♯m
F♯m(maj7)
F♯m7
B7
So, they turn a - round__ and go,__ leave her by the ra - di - o.__
D
A/C♯
Bm7
She did - n't love 'em an - y - way, not like she loves__ the men__
E7sus
Chorus:
Am7
__ who play. She loves to hear__ the mu - sic,
cresc.

E7/G♯
Am/G
she's got ev - 'ry lyr - ic down.
She loves to hear them sing, she's got the great-
F♯m7(♭5)
D9
Dm7
Em7
est ears in town.
You'll find her at the stu - di - o,
Dm7
Em7
Am
G
the first to come, the last to go.
Some - times, they take her home,
Fmaj7
Dm7
Em7
Am
but she al - ways wakes up a - lone.
A - lone,

G♯dim7
Am/G
F♯m7(♭5)
a - lone,
a-lone.
Bridge:
Fmaj7
G/F
Em7
A7(♭9)
She could have been some - bod - y's wife,
but as a child, heard "Mack The Knife,"
Dm7
Em7
Fmaj7
Dm7
Em7
and each time she took it home.
So, she'll al - ways wake up a - lone.
Chorus:
A
G
Cm
'Cause she loves to hear the mu - sic, she's got

G7sus
G7
E♭7
ev - 'ry lyr - ic down. And she loves to hear them sing, she's got the
F9
A♭/B♭
E♭
great - est ears in town. Don't you know that she loves to hear the mu-
G7
Cm
sic. Oh, she loves to hear the mu-
F9
A♭/B♭
E♭
sic. Won't some - bod - y put an - oth - er nick - el in,

G7
Cm
in the nick-el - o - de-on and let her hear mu - sic.
Oh, mu-
F9
A♭/B♭
E♭
sic.
Oh, she loves it,
she loves to hear
G7
Cm
F9
it.
Let me hear some mu - sic.
She loves to hear,
rit.
Cm9
she loves to hear
the mu - sic.

SURE THING, BABY

Words and Music by
PETER ALLEN

Moderately ♩ = 100

Bm7
Am9
E7sus
kay. But what a-bout to - day? Look a - round
Verse 2:
A(9)
Bm/A
as the old stars make way for the dawn.
C♯m7
Ev - 'ry - one says, "No time like the pres - ent." And if they're
Bm7
Gmaj7
Cmaj7/G
right, what a-bout to - night? If you play your mu - sic

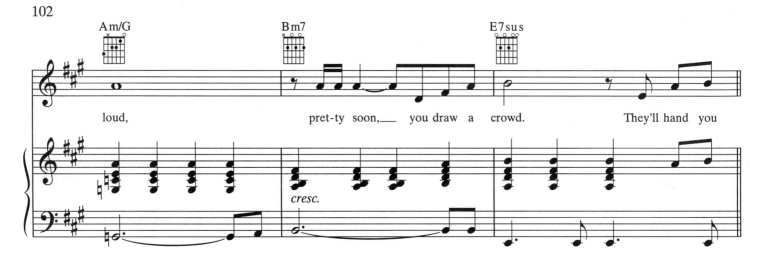

Am/G Bm7 E7sus

loud, pret-ty soon, you draw a crowd. They'll hand you

cresc.

F♯m7 Bm7 E7sus E7

life on a plat - ter and when you're gone, what does it

A(9) C♯7 F♯m7 B7 A/B B7

mat - ter, an - y - how? 'Cause the on - ly time

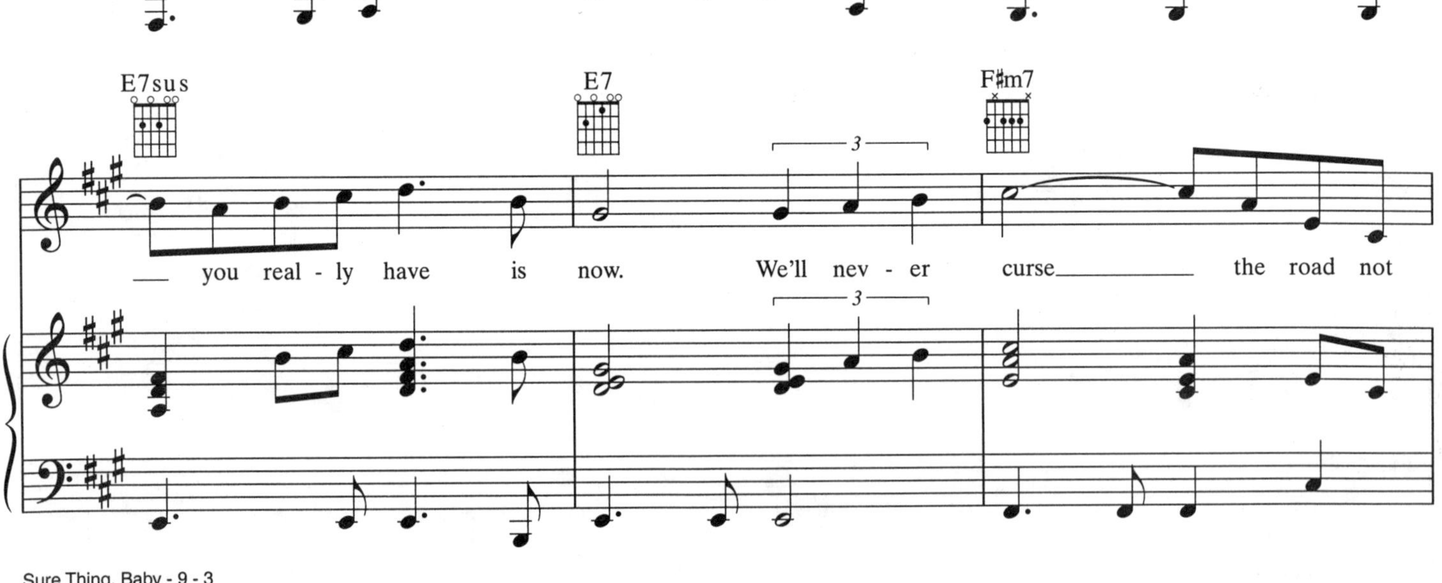

E7sus
E7
F♯m7
you real - ly have is now. We'll nev - er curse the road not

Bm7 E7sus E7 A(9) C♯7

tak - en. Don't fall a - sleep, just stay a - wake and see the

F♯m7 F♯m(maj7) A/B B7 E7sus

sun. I may not know much, but I know my day___ has be -

A(9) E7sus

gun.

Chorus:

Gm7

Give me a chance_ to

Cm7 F9 B♭maj7

be some - bod - y. A hun - dred to one I can re - pay.___

Bm7
E7sus
E7
Am7
What are the odds a - gainst to - mor - row be - ing my day?
Am7
Bm7
Cmaj7
D
F♯m7
Bm7
Sure thing, ba - by.
B♭m7
E♭7sus
E♭7
A♭(9)
3
When you're
dim.
mp
Verse 3:
B♭m/A♭
down, ev - 'ry-thing looks im - pos - si - bly high.

Cm7
B♭m7
What could a guy like me get to hope for? A job? A wife? What a-bout a
A♭m9
E♭7sus
E7sus
Verse 4:
A(9)
life? So, you see that
Bm/A
e-ven if you're a no one like me, when the time fi-n'lly comes, run and
C♯m7
D
Gmaj7
catch it. No mat-ter when, it won't come a - gain.

Cmaj7/G
Am/G
Bm7
Fly your flags and ban - ners high.
Write your name a - cross the
cresc.
Chorus:
E7sus
Am7
Dm7
sky. And just give me a chance to be some - bod - y.
mf
G7sus
G7
Cmaj7
C♯m7
Hun-dred to one I can re - pay.
What are the odds a - gainst
F♯7sus
F♯7
Bm7
C♯m7
Dmaj7
E7
to - mor - row be - ing my day?
Sure thing, ba - by.

Gm7
Cm7
F7sus
F7
Life on a plat - ter. When you're gone, what does it
Bb(9)
D7
Gm7
C7
Bb/C
C7
mat - ter an - y - how? 'Cause the on - ly time
F7sus
F7
Gm7
you real - ly have is now. We'll nev - er curse the road not
Cm7
F7sus
F7
Bb(9)
D7
tak - en. Don't fall a - sleep, just stay a - wake and see the

Gm7 Gm(maj7) B♭/C C7 Cm7 Dm7
sun. I may not know much but I know my day
E♭maj7 F7sus F♯dim7 Gm7 B♭/C C7
has be - gun.
E♭/F Dm/F E♭/F F B♭sus E♭/B♭ B♭
My day has be - gun.
rit.

TENTERFIELD SADDLER

Words and Music by
PETER ALLEN

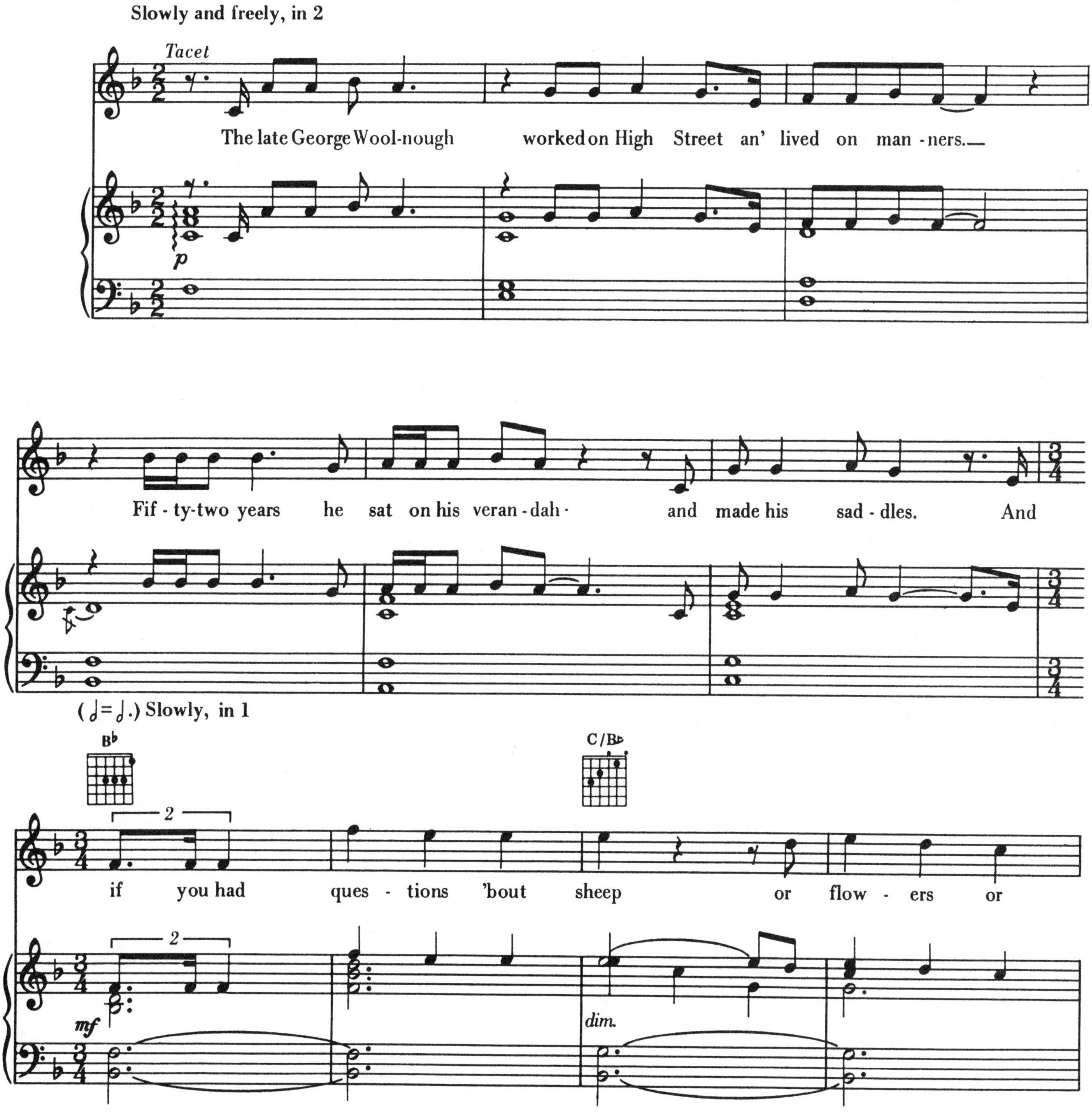

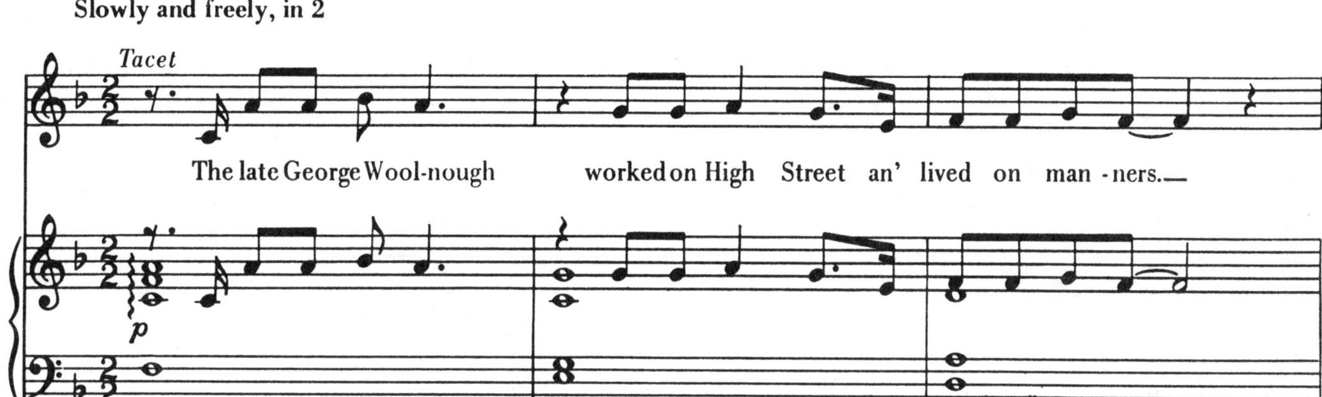

Slowly and freely, in 2
Tacet
The late George Wool-nough worked on High Street an' lived on man - ners.
p
Fif - ty-two years he sat on his veran - dah - and made his sad - dles. And
(𝅗𝅥 = 𝅗𝅥.) Slowly, in 1
B♭
C/B♭
if you had ques - tions 'bout sheep or flow - ers or
mf
dim.

Am7
C/D
dogs,
you'd just ask the
mp
C11
C7
Sad - ler.
He lived with - out sin; they're
C7sus 4
F
build - ing a li - br'y for him.
F
Time is a trav - el - er, Ten - ter - field Sad - d - ler

C11
C7
turn your head.
C11
Gm7
C11
Ride a - gain, jack - a - roo; think I see kan - ga - roo
F
up a - head.
F
C/E
The son of George Wool-nough went off and got
mf

Dm
B♭
mar-ried, and had a war ba - by.
Though some-thing was wrong
F/A
C
and it's eas-i-er to drink than go cra - zy.
B♭
C/B♭
And if there were ques-tions a-bout why the
Am7
Dm7
end was so sad,
well,

C11
C7
George had no an - swers a - bout why a son
C7sus 4
F
ev - er has need of a gun.
F
Time is a trav - el - er, Ten - ter - field
Gm7
C11
Gm7
Sad - d - ler, turn your head.

C11
Gm7
C11
Ride a - gain, jack - a - roo; think I see
F
kan - ga - roo up a - head.
Cm7(add F)
F
C
The grand - son of George has been all a - round the
f

A7/C♯
Dm
world and lives no spe - cial place,
B♭
F/C
changed his last name and he mar - ried a girl
C/E
with an in - t'rest - ing face.
B♭
C/B♭
He'd al - most for - got - ten them both be -

Am7
Dm7
cause in the life___ that he leads there's
C11
C7
C11
no - where for George and his li - br'y or the son with his gun___
mp
Dm/A
Gm7
___ to be - long ex - cept in this
C11
F
Repeat (vocal ad lib) and fade
song.___ Time is a trav - el - er, Ten - ter - field
mf
Repeat and fade

Vocal Ad Lib

Time is a meddler,
Tenterfield Saddler,
Make your bed.
Fly away, cockatoo;
Down on the ground emu
Up ahead.

WHEN I GET MY NAME IN LIGHTS

Words and Music by
PETER ALLEN

F7+
Dm7♭5
G7
for - tune and fame,
When you get your name in lights,
C
F7
Fm7
It can hap - pen ov - er - night in these mod - ern times.
B♭7
E♭
C7
F7
Here in the jazz age the
B♭
Dm7
G7
E7♭5
B♭7°
world is at a cra - zy stage.
You can be fa - mous and

A7
Dm7
G7
F♯7♯11
F7
cause a pan - ic, If you slick back your hair and then you fly the At - lan - tic.
B♭
F7+
And that's why I won't let go 'til I'm on ra - di - o. And
Dm7♭5
G7
C7
when they come to see the sights, that - 'll be my name spelt right
F7
Fm7
B♭
3
light - ing Old Times Square. I'll

Gm
Gmmaj7
Gm7
sit on a flag - pole, what - ev - er the rage, Just to get my mug - sy on the

C9
F#7
Bb/F
Eb6/F
front page, Just to get my name

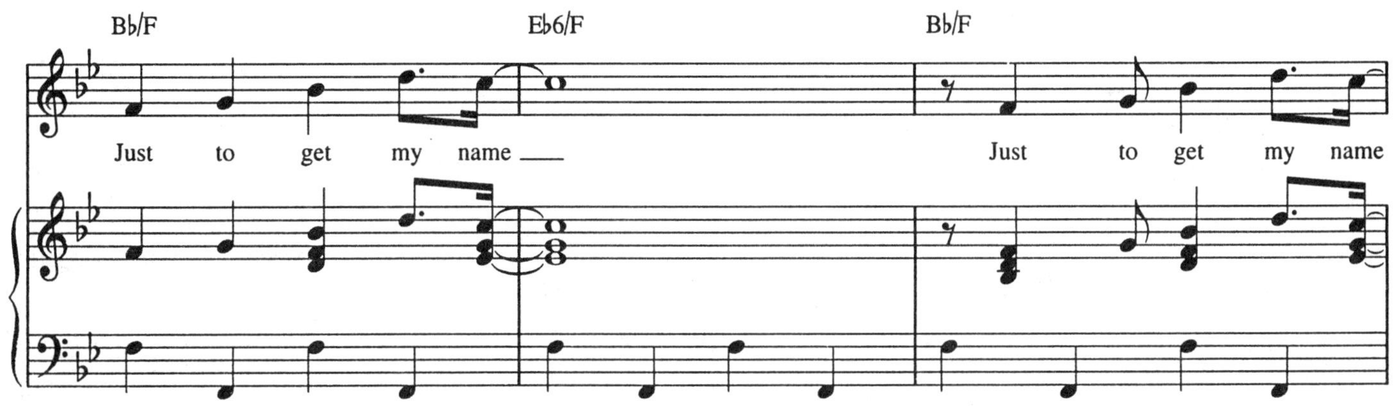
Bb/F
Eb6/F
Bb/F
Just to get my name Just to get my name

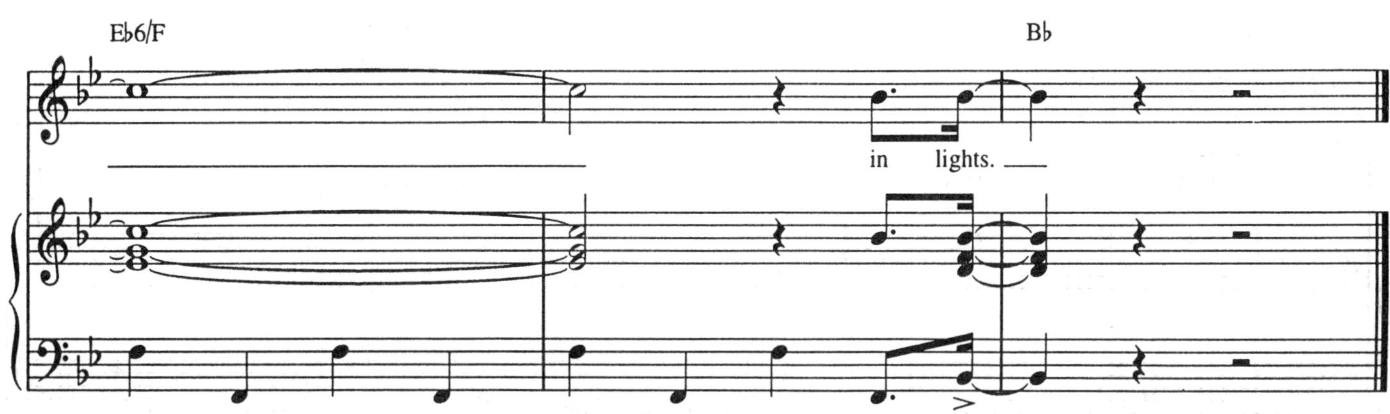
Eb6/F
Bb
in lights.

YOU AND ME
(We Wanted It All)

Words and Music by
CAROLE BAYER SAGER and PETER ALLEN

Am7
To Coda
1. Am7/D
2.3. Am7/D
we want - ed it al - ways. eyes.
Chorus: E(add 9)
C♯m7
F♯m7
B9
Look how all our dreams came true, see how I've got
mf
Emaj7
C♯m7
F♯m7
F♯m7/B
B9/A
me, and ba - by, you've got you.
G♯m7
C♯m7
F♯m7
F♯m7/B
Through it all just one thing died, a lit - tle thing called

Verse 2:
You and me, we reached for the sky, the limit was high;
Never giving in, certain we could win that prize;
I should have seen it in your eyes. (To Chorus:)

Verse 3:
You and me, we're not like the rest, we once were the best;
Back when we were dumb, how did we become so smart,
And learn to break each other's heart? (To Chorus:)

Verse 4:
You and me, we're not like the rest, we once were the best,
But look what we became, isn't it a crying shame,
That we almost . . (To Coda:)